EXTREME PLACES

The Highest Mountain

Other books in the Extreme Places series include:

EXTREME PLACES

The Highest Mountain

Kris Hirschmann

KIDHAVEN PRESS™

San Diego • Detroit • New York • San Francisco • Cleveland
New Haven, Conn. • Waterville, Maine • London • Munich

THOMSON

GALE

Cover photo: © Galen Rowell/CORBIS
© AFP/CORBIS, 42, 43
© Andrews, Michael/Minden Pictures, 7
Associated Press, AP, 23, 39
Associated Press, The Grand Island Independent, 37
© Corel Corporation, 10
© Tim Fitzharris/Minden Pictures, 13
© Simon Fraser/Science Source/Photo Researchers, 20
© Tim Hauf Photography/Visuals Unlimited Inc., 18, 40
Hulton/Archive by Getty Images, 14, 22, 32, 34
© NASA/Visuals Unlimited Inc., 25
Brandy Noon, 9, 17
Photos12.com, 29, 30
© Galen Rowell/CORBIS, 27
© Kevin Schafer/CORBIS, 12

For more information, contact
KidHaven Press
27500 Drake Rd.
Farmington Hills, MI 48331-3535
Or you can visit our Internet site at http://www.gale.com

LIBRARY OF CONGRESS CATALOGING-IN-PUBLICATION DATA

Hirschmann, Kris, 1967–
    The highest mountain / by Kris Hirschmann.
       p. cm. — (Extreme places)
Summary: Describes the geography, climate, animals and plants, measurement,
exploration, and ecology of Mount Everest.
Includes bibliographical references and index.
    ISBN 0-7377-1373-9 (hardback : alk. paper)
    1. Everest, Mount (China and Nepal)—Juvenile literature. [1. Everest, Mount
(China and Nepal) 2. Mountaineering.] I. Title. II, Series.
    DS495.8.E9 H57 2003
    915.496—dc21

                                                2002007596

Contents

The Top of the World

The world's highest mountain is Mount Everest. Located on the border of Nepal and Tibet, this mighty peak rises 29,035 feet (more than five and a half miles) into the sky.

With its towering slopes and snowy top, Everest is one of the most impressive sights on Earth. The mountain's local names reflect this fact. In Nepal, Mount Everest is called Sagarmatha, which means "goddess of the sky." Everest's Tibetan name is Chomolungma, which means "mother goddess of the world."

The Himalayan Range

Mount Everest is part of the Himalayan mountain range. "Himalaya" is a Sanskrit word that means "abode of snow." This name came from Indian pilgrims who traveled through the area long ago. It refers to the cold upper regions of the mountain range, where snow never melts.

The Himalayan range stretches in an east-west arc from Pakistan to Bhutan. In between, it also passes through India, Nepal, Tibet, and Sikkim. The entire range is about 1,500 miles long, and its width ranges from 60 to 250 miles. The range covers an area of about 230,000 square miles.

Home to some of the highest mountain peaks in the world, the Himalayas stretch across 1,500 miles.

Scientists divide the Himalayas into four parts: the Outer Himalaya to the south, the Great Himalaya to the north, the Lesser Himalaya in the middle, and the Tibetan Himalaya in Tibet. The Great Himalaya has an average **elevation** of about 20,000 feet. It is the highest region on Earth. Many of the world's tallest peaks are found here. These include Everest, Kangchenjunga (28,169 feet), Lhotse (27,923 feet), and Makalu (27,766 feet).

Growth of the Himalayas

The process that created these massive mountains is called **continental drift.** Continental drift involves seven separate plates that make up the earth's crust. In some places the plates are spreading apart. In other places they are being pushed together. The movement is slow (most plates shift just a couple of inches each year), but it is steady. Over long periods of time, the earth's plates move enough to make entire continents "drift" from one place to another.

The Himalayas were born between 60 and 100 million years ago when the land mass that is now India drifted into Asia. India was moving northward at a rate of about six inches per year. When it bumped into Asia, pressure from the collision shoved huge amounts of rocky debris upward. Over millions of years the Indian plate kept pushing, and the debris pile kept growing. At the same time, the edge of the Asian plate wrinkled into hills. The wrinkles and the debris got higher and higher. They eventually reached mountain height, and the Himalayas were born.

Over time the movement of the Indian plate has slowed. Today it is moving at a rate of about two inches

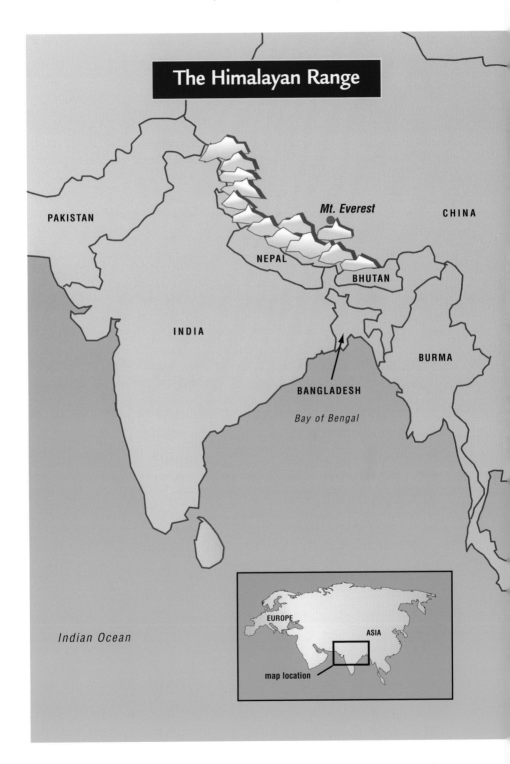

The Himalayan Range

PAKISTAN

Mt. Everest

CHINA

NEPAL

BHUTAN

INDIA

BURMA

BANGLADESH

Bay of Bengal

Indian Ocean

EUROPE

ASIA

map location

The Himalayas grow about two inches taller every year.

per year. But the plate is still pushing against Asia. As a result, Everest and the rest of the Himalayas continue to grow. Scientists believe that Mount Everest is rising about one-half inch each year. But the mountain will not keep getting taller forever. Earthquakes, **erosion**, and other natural forces will continue to change the height of Everest and the other Himalayan peaks in unpredictable ways.

Weather Conditions

The climate of Mount Everest is fairly predictable. Although the timing changes a little bit from year to year, there are generally three seasons in the Mount Everest area. There is a cold period from October through February, a warmer period from March through mid-June, and a rainy season from mid-June through September.

A consistent climate, however, does not mean consistent conditions. Everest's extreme height leads to very different weather on different parts of the mountain. The lower parts of Everest get moderate temperatures and plenty of rain. The upper parts of the mountain, on the other hand, experience freezing weather all year long. Temperatures as low as minus forty degrees Fahrenheit have been recorded, and snow never leaves the ground.

The upper regions of Mount Everest may also experience blinding snowstorms with hurricane-strength winds of 125 miles per hour or even more. These storms can whip up in a matter of hours and may last for days. They are especially common during the autumn rainy season.

Life at Lower Elevations

Mount Everest's many weather zones create different living conditions for many interesting plants and animals. The richest area is found below 8,000 feet. In these lower regions, summertime temperatures average a pleasant seventy degrees Fahrenheit and rainfall is plentiful. As a result, the forests around Everest's base grow thick. Pine and hemlock are the most common trees in the very lowest regions. Silver fir and birch trees begin to appear near the 8,000-foot mark. Many types of wildflowers, grasses, and shrubs also grow throughout this region.

The forests of the lower regions provide food and shelter for many species of animals. The endangered

Himalayan black bear, for example, lives at the very lowest levels of Mount Everest. This rare animal averages 250 pounds in weight and 5 feet in length. It prefers heavily wooded areas and usually stays below 5,000 feet.

The lower forests are also home to many smaller mammals including langurs (a type of monkey), jackals, and weasels. More than one hundred species of birds and hundreds of different types of insects can also be found in the thick woods surrounding Mount Everest.

The Himalayan black bear is native to the forests that lie at the foot of Mount Everest.

Animals on the Upper Mountain

Moving up the mountain, weather conditions begin to change. The temperature drops three and a half degrees for every one thousand feet of elevation. The air also holds less and less oxygen as elevation increases. Rainfall drops off, and wind and storm activity pick up.

Animal life changes along with the weather. The regions above 8,000 feet support hardy animals that can deal with the harsh conditions on Everest's higher slopes. One such animal is the danphe, a colorful pheasant found from about 10,000 feet up to 13,000 feet. This bird is the national symbol of Nepal, and it is common on Everest. Danphe can often be seen scratching and pecking at the ground as they hunt for seeds, roots, small mammals, and insect larvae.

A little higher on Everest lives the Himalayan musk deer. The musk deer stands less than 2 feet tall and weighs just 30 pounds, and it can be found at elevations as high as 14,200 feet. Musk deer have long front teeth that stick out of their mouths like fangs. They are hunted for their musk glands, which contain a substance that is used to make perfumes and medicines.

Snow leopards also exist in the highest parts of Everest and can sometimes be found roaming above 19,000 feet.

The Himalayan tahr (a type of mountain goat) lives at around the same elevation as the musk deer. The tahr stands about 3 feet tall and weighs up to 190 pounds. It has a thick, woolly coat to protect it from the cold weather high on the mountain, and it has bendable hooves that give it a good grip on rocky surfaces. Males sometimes fight by butting heads, and they have two thick, curved horns that help them during battle.

Viewed from 18,500 feet, Mount Everest's western shoulder scrapes the sky, with Mount Nuptse to the left.

The only large mammal that sometimes roams above 19,000 feet during the warmest parts of the summer is the snow leopard. Snow leopards may grow up to 3 feet long, not including the tail, and may weigh as much as 120 pounds. They have thick coats of pale gray fur with black spots. The pelt of the snow leopard is highly prized for use in coats and other fur products. As a result, snow leopards are now endangered. On Everest, these rare animals are seldom seen.

Changes in Plant Life

Changing weather conditions affect more than just the animal life on Everest. They change the plant life, too. From 8,000 to 10,000 feet, the spreading trees of the base forests die off and tough, small trees like junipers and rhododendrons take over. Above 12,500 feet, trees disappear altogether. Only shrubs and grasses grow this high on the mountain. Above 16,500 feet, lichen and mosses are the only plant life. And growth ceases altogether at about 18,800 feet. Past this point (called the **snowline**) Everest is so cold that snow covers the ground all year long.

Above the snowline Mount Everest is a barren wasteland of snow, ice, and rocks. Neither plants nor animals can survive for long on the frigid, storm-whipped upper mountain. Everest may be one of the most magnificent places on Earth—but it is also one of the harshest.

Measuring the Mountain

Mount Everest was declared the world's tallest mountain in 1852, when the first measurement was completed. Since that time many other tall mountains have been found and measured. None, however, has been able to beat Everest's record-breaking height. And scientists have now measured all of the world's major peaks, so Everest's record will stand until the earth's movements either pull Everest down or push another peak upward.

Declaring Everest the world's tallest mountain was easy. Finding its actual height, however, was not. The first measurement of Everest involved many scientists and years of mathematical calculations, and the result was full of errors. Over the years scientific knowledge and technology improved, and more precise work became possible. It took 150 years and many measurements to arrive at Everest's current official height of 29,035 feet.

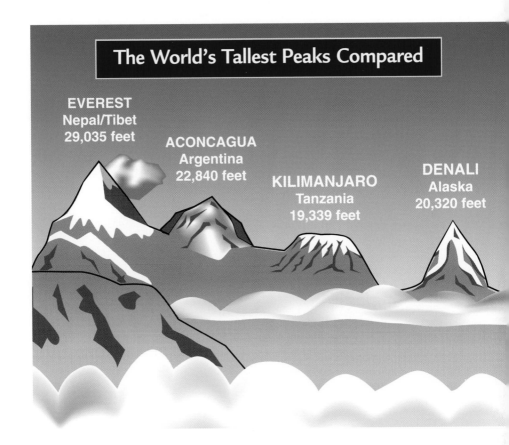

The World's Tallest Peaks Compared

EVEREST
Nepal/Tibet
29,035 feet

ACONCAGUA
Argentina
22,840 feet

KILIMANJARO
Tanzania
19,339 feet

DENALI
Alaska
20,320 feet

Preparing to Measure

The first measurement of Mount Everest was carried out by a huge British-led mapping project called the Grand Trigonometrical Survey of India. Measurement efforts began in 1847, when scientists mapping other Himalayan mountains first noticed Everest's remote and snowy peak. These scientists thought Everest (which was then un-named) looked taller than the mountains around it. They decided to measure the mysterious peak.

A mountain's height is the distance its **summit** (highest point) rises above sea level. But Mount Everest is far from the ocean, and its base (lowest point) is thousands

A majestic view of the Himalayas is revealed from the Solu-Khumbu trek in Nepal.

of feet above sea level. So to measure Everest, scientists first had to find the exact elevation of the mountain's base. They did this by "carrying in" sea level. Starting at the ocean's edge, teams of scientists walked thousands of miles toward Mount Everest. They recorded elevation changes along the way.

Under normal circumstances, the scientists would have walked all the way to the base of Mount Everest. Then they would have added all the elevation changes to see how far up they had traveled before trying to measure the mountain. But in the mid-1800s, getting to Everest's base was a problem. At that time Tibet and Nepal were closed to foreigners. Therefore scientists could not carry sea level all the way to Mount Everest. They had to stop as much as 150 miles from the base of the mountain.

Sir Andrew Waugh, who then headed the Grand Trigonometrical Survey, knew that this great distance would make any measurement less accurate. So he sent many teams of scientists to approach the mountain from different angles. By averaging multiple measurements, Sir Andrew hoped to get the most accurate possible figure for Everest's height.

Many Measurements

Sir Andrew's teams of scientists got as close to Everest as they could. Then they set up instruments called **theodolites**, which are special telescopes that calculate angles. Each team sighted the tip of Mount Everest through its theodolite. The scientists then read from a gauge that showed them the exact angle of the theodolite's barrel. By plugging this angle into a complicated mathematical equation, scientists could find the height of Everest's peak.

The process sounds simple, but it was not. Each team working around Everest came up with a different measurement. So many measurements meant a lot more work—and a lot more math. The results of each survey had to be found. Then all the results had to be combined to create a final answer. The calculation process was done by hand and took several years to complete. In 1852, when all the work was finally done, scientists announced the final height of Mount Everest: 29,002 feet.

Theodolites, which were used to determine the height of Mount Everest in the 1850s, are used here by surveyors at the edge of the Arctic Ocean.

Shortly after this number was announced, Britain's Royal Geographic Society named the newly measured peak in honor of Sir George Everest. Everest headed the Trigonometrical Survey from 1823 to 1843. Although Sir George did not help to measure Mount Everest, his work laid the foundation for this important project.

Mistakes Made

The Trigonometrical Survey's results were disputed almost from the beginning. No one doubted that Everest was the world's tallest mountain, but scientists did complain that the Survey had made mistakes. The biggest concern was that the British survey had not accounted for two important factors: **refraction** (the bending of light) and gravity.

Refraction occurs when light passes through air of different thicknesses and temperatures. The different air layers actually cause light beams to bend a little bit. As a result, objects viewed from a distance might not be where they seem to be. Since Everest's height was originally measured from great distances, scientists argued that the peak might have been sighted incorrectly due to refraction.

Scientists also felt that gravity had not been properly considered. Mountains are so huge and heavy that they have their own gravitational pull. If scientific instruments are not adjusted for this pull, they will give wrong readings. Many believed that these types of errors had been made in the original survey.

The arguments raged for more than a century. Finally, in 1953, an Indian team set out to remeasure Mount Everest. The team was able to get much closer to the mountain since foreigners were now allowed on Everest. Also, the Indian scientists used the most modern methods of the day to avoid the mistakes made by the British. The Indian survey was completed in 1954 and a new, more accurate height of Everest was announced: 29,028 feet.

The Current Official Height

The Indian figure was accepted as Everest's official height for many decades. By the mid-1990s, however, scientists began to think that it was time for another measurement. New technologies promised more accurate numbers than ever before. Also, climbers now had the knowledge

Members of the 1953 Everest expedition test their equipment on the Tryfan, a three-thousand-foot peak in Snowdonia, Wales.

and equipment to climb Mount Everest. Neither the Trigonometrical Survey nor the Indian scientists had been able to do this. So in 1999 an international team of scientists sponsored by the National Geographic Society set out to measure the mountain once again.

A satellite captured this image of Camp One, as a member of the 1999 Everest expedition team attempts to cross a three-ladder bridge.

The new team climbed to the tip of Mount Everest. Once on the summit, the scientists used a revolutionary new technology called **GPS** to find Everest's height. GPS stands for global positioning system. It works by beaming information to satellites in orbit around the earth. Several satellites compare the information they receive and return data to the GPS receiver. The receiver then calculates its own precise position, including elevation.

Using this method, the National Geographic scientists came up with yet another height for Mount Everest. The new number was 29,035 feet. This figure is considered to be the best measurement ever made of Everest, and today it is accepted as the mountain's official height.

Margin of Error

Scientists agree, however, that even the current number may not be correct. Like any technology, GPS has limits. In particular, GPS numbers are based on a receiver's distance from the center of the planet. A mountain's height, on the other hand, is based on sea level—and sea level is not the same everywhere on Earth. Local gravity and other factors change this important measurement from place to place.

Although GPS technology finds locations with pinpoint accuracy, it cannot calculate sea level. Scientists have to figure that out themselves. This process is difficult, especially in mountainous areas. Experts admit that estimates of the sea level under Everest may be off by several feet. And if the estimate is wrong, then the calculated height of Everest is wrong, too—even when measured with GPS technology.

This bird's-eye view of the Himalayas was recorded by a NASA satellite.

Today, world mapping organizations are working to find better ways of measuring sea level in areas like the Himalayas. Until they succeed, the exact heights of Mount Everest and other tall peaks of the world will not be known.

Reaching the Peak

Climbing to the summit of Mount Everest is difficult and dangerous. Yet hundreds of people make the attempt each year. With its towering peak and extreme conditions, Everest presents a challenge to many **mountaineers.**

The history of climbing attempts on Mount Everest is full of excitement and triumph. It is also full of tragedy. But to mountaineers, the potential for disaster is part of Everest's appeal. If the climb were not so hard, success would not taste so sweet.

Early Attempts

The first attempt to reach Everest's summit was made in 1921. A British team of eight climbers and scientists set off for the mountain in May of that year. By September the team had reached a height of about 22,000 feet—but

Perched on a steep slope, an ice climber makes his way up Mount Everest.

it would go no farther. Winter was approaching, and extreme cold put a halt to the expedition before the climbers could reach the top of Everest.

Although the first expedition did not reach the summit, it did inspire other climbers. Many other groups tried to reach the summit over the next few decades. But all of the expeditions ran into trouble. Some groups were stopped by falling ice or avalanches. (In 1922, an Everest avalanche killed seven climbers.) Other groups lost members to cold and illness. And all groups had to deal with Everest's freezing conditions. High on the mountain, the windchill may plunge to –150 degrees Fahrenheit. This is cold enough to freeze skin instantly. Such conditions forced many expeditions to turn back before reaching the summit.

At least one early group experienced an even more extreme side of Mount Everest. Two members of a 1924 expedition were climbing toward Everest's summit on a crystal-clear day when a blizzard suddenly blew in. The surprise storm pounded the mountain with hurricane-strength winds for two hours before clearing. When the clouds rolled away, the climbers had disappeared. Their bodies were never found.

Thin Air

Stormy weather, freezing temperatures, and difficult **terrain** are not the only obstacles to climbing Everest. Thinning air on the world's highest mountain is also a problem.

Even at lower levels, the air on Everest is thin enough to make breathing difficult. And things get worse as a

Members of the 1922 Everest expedition, who were able to reach a height of 22,000 feet before harsh conditions forced them back.

climber moves up the mountain. The air gets thinner and thinner, and climbers find it harder and harder to breathe. Conditions become extreme near Everest's summit. There the air holds only one-third as much oxygen as it does at sea level. This is barely enough oxygen to keep a person alive.

Early climbers dealt with the falling oxygen levels by ascending just a couple of thousand feet per day. At the end of each day, the climbers rested at high-altitude camps to let their bodies adjust. By rising a little bit at a time, climbers got used to the changing air and were able to function at higher and higher altitudes. This process is called **acclimatization**, and it is still used by climbers today.

Early climbers would soon discover, however, that even acclimatization could not help them above 26,000 feet. The very thin air at this level starves the brain of oxygen. A

29

person in this state becomes very confused. A person also pants constantly as his or her body struggles to suck oxygen from the air. The panting causes water loss, or **dehydration**. Dehydration leads to weakness and severe coughing. By the time a climber nears Everest's summit, exhaustion sets in. Even the simplest movements become difficult. Climbers may take one step, for example, then stand still for several minutes trying to catch their breath. At this point, every movement is a mental and physical challenge.

Today, most climbers use modern oxygen-supplying equipment to help them breathe high on Mount Everest. Most early climbers also used oxygen. But the oxygen tanks and gear available in the early 1900s were heavy and awkward. A climber's oxygen pack might weigh more than forty pounds. (By contrast, modern oxygen gear weighs as little as seven pounds.) Also, the gear did not work very well. It often failed at high altitudes. Without a comfortable, dependable oxygen supply, early mountaineers had a tough time reaching the higher levels of Mount Everest.

First Success

Despite the many difficulties of climbing Everest, the expeditions kept coming. In 1953 one finally succeeded.

The 1953 expedition was organized by Great Britain, and it included ten climbers. The group reached the base of Everest in late March and immediately started moving up the mountain. Camps were pitched at 20,150 feet, 21,200 feet, 22,000 feet, and 23,000 feet. For several weeks

Sherpas weigh baggage just prior to the Hillary expedition.

the climbers moved up and down between the four camps to let their bodies adjust to the thin air. In May a final camp was pitched at 27,900 feet. Climbers would

Camp Chang-la served as a temporary home for the members of the 1922 Everest expedition.

spend the night at this high camp, then push for the summit the following morning.

On May 28 five climbers set out for the high camp. Each climber was loaded with about fifty pounds of supplies, including oxygen tanks. All 250 pounds' worth of supplies would be needed to help two of the climbers reach Everest's summit the following morning. The two were a young New Zealander named Edmund Hillary and Nepalese climber named Tenzing Norgay.

After many hard hours of climbing the team reached the high camp. The three supply carriers left their packs and returned down the mountain. Hillary and Tenzing settled in for the night. The two men opened oxygen tanks inside their tents to help them breathe. They also drank gallons of hot tea to replace the body liquids they were losing in the thin, cold air.

The Summit

At 6:30 A.M. on May 29, Hillary and Tenzing lifted oxygen tanks onto their backs and set out for the summit. The climb was hard work because the crusty snow kept breaking under the climbers' weight. Over and over, Hillary and Tenzing dug themselves out of snow pits as they made their way up the mountain.

Higher and higher the climbers went, far higher than anyone had ever gone before. But the weather was perfect and the climbers' oxygen tanks were working well. So the two men moved steadily upward. At 11:30 A.M. they mounted one final hill and discovered that there was nothing left to climb. Hillary and Tenzing had become

Tenzing Norgay (left) and Edmund Hillary (right) arrive in London after becoming the first men to climb the world's highest mountain.

the first people on Earth to stand on the summit of Mount Everest.

Others Follow

The British expedition may have been the first to reach the top of Mount Everest, but others would soon follow. The Swiss summitted in 1956, just three years after

Hillary, and the Chinese made it in 1960. The Americans followed in 1963 and the Indians in 1965. With each success, the route discovered by Hillary and Tenzing became a little more familiar to the world's climbing community. And the number of mountaineers trying to reach Everest's summit grew steadily over the years.

Today hundreds of climbers attempt Everest each year, and many succeed. In the 1990s alone, 882 people stood on top of the world's highest mountain. Even for the best climbers, though, Mount Everest is a challenge. Conditions on the mountain are just as severe as they were in the early days of Everest expeditions, and people still die. But this does not stop climbers from flocking to Mount Everest. To mountaineers, the danger is just one more thing that makes Everest special.

The World's Highest Dump

T he highest parts of the Himalayas are among the
most unspoiled places on Earth, mostly because few
people can get there. Many people *do* live in the lower regions, but most Himalayan settlements are rural. They
create very little pollution. The high altitudes and lack of
industry in the area have protected these magnificent
mountains.

A few specific areas, however, are suffering from the
presence of humans. Mount Everest is one of these areas.
Tourist traffic on and around Everest increases every year,
and this activity has taken a toll on the health of the
mountain.

The Problem with Tourism

In the earliest days of Everest exploration, the Nepalese
and Tibetan governments restricted foreign visitors.

Climbing expeditions needed permits, and only one or two permits were issued each year. So just a few climbers set foot on Everest each season, and little damage was done to the environment.

In later years, however, government policies relaxed and more permits were issued. Two new airstrips in the Everest region also made it easier for foreigners to reach the remote area. Between these two developments, tourist traffic picked up. The number of visitors increased each decade from the 1950s onward. By the end

An increased amount of tourism to Nepal and Tibet in recent years has led to an environmental crisis.

of the 1990s thousands of people were flocking to Everest each year. Some of these visitors intended to climb Everest. Others came to trek in the lower regions of the mountain. All needed food, fuel, places to stay, and more.

Local people started to use up the area's natural resources to serve the growing number of tourists. The biggest effect was on Everest's forests. Huge numbers of trees were cut down and sold to climbing expeditions to be burned as firewood. Trees also provided the wood needed to build new hotels, bars, and shops. Once opened, these businesses required more wood for cooking and heat. The tourists kept coming and the demand for wood kept increasing.

This situation has had a serious effect on the Everest environment. Mostly because of the tourist trade, land that was once covered with thick forests is now bare. Scientists estimate that 20 to 40 percent of Everest's forests have been lost since the 1950s.

Garbage on the Mountain

Litter is another big problem on Everest. Climbing expeditions take an average of fifteen thousand pounds of supplies up Everest, but they do not bring everything back down. Trash is heavy and hard to pack out, so most expeditions just do not bother. Instead, they dump their garbage all over the mountain. The problem is so bad that Mount Everest is sometimes called the highest junkyard in the world.

Base Camp, the area where most expeditions gather before heading up the mountain, is the worst spot. Food

A team of recyclers crushes aluminum cans at the base camp of Mount Everest in 1998.

packaging, broken tents, empty oxygen bottles, human waste, medical waste, and many other types of junk are scattered throughout the area. Garbage does not rot away in the thin, cold air high on Everest. This means that any mess made at Base Camp remains until someone carries it back down the mountain.

There is plenty of garbage higher on Everest, too. Climbers dump used oxygen bottles, food wrappers, and other unneeded items as they make their way to and from

A lonely monument stands at the Solu-Khumbu trek in Nepal as a memorial to all those who have perished climbing Mount Everest. Some of these bodies still lie on the mountain.

Everest's summit. Like the debris at Base Camp, these objects do not break down over time. They stay on top of the mountain, littering the path for future climbers.

One more gruesome form of litter can also be found on Mount Everest: the bodies of dead climbers. At high altitudes, living climbers are so tired, cold, and weak that they cannot drag heavy corpses down the mountain or even away from the main climbing route. More than 170 people have lost their lives on Everest, and some of these people's corpses lie right in the middle of the trail. Climbers must walk over the frozen bodies as they make their way up and down the mountain.

Keeping It Clean

Everest's litter problem is not new. Dead bodies and garbage have been piling up on the mountain since the 1950s. The situation drew little attention until the 1990s. Finally, however, the pollution became too severe to ignore any longer. So the Nepalese government introduced new rules for climbers. In 1992 the government raised the Everest expedition fee from ten thousand dollars to fifty thousand dollars per group. It also decided to issue fewer climbing permits each year. The government hoped that these two changes would reduce the number of climbers—and the amount of trash—on Everest.

More recently, the government began collecting a four-thousand-dollar "cleanliness deposit" from visiting expeditions. The deposit is lost if climbers do not bring their trash down from the mountain. The Nepalese government hopes that this fee will encourage climbers to carry their garbage out instead of scattering it across Mount Everest.

Private groups have also taken steps to help Mount Everest, mostly by sending cleanup crews onto the mountain. An organization called the Sagarmatha Environmental Expedition (SEE), for example, has taken more than seventeen thousand pounds of garbage off Everest since 1994. Four Everest Environmental Expeditions have hauled out more than one thousand empty oxygen bottles plus several tons of additional trash since 1995. These and other cleanup groups have helped to reduce Mount Everest's litter problem.

The most important cleanup effort, however, is being made by the climbers themselves. Today the world climbing community is very aware of Mount Everest's pollution problems. As a result, Everest visitors are taking care not to harm the environment. More climbers than ever before are packing out their garbage. Many expeditions also have strict rules for handling garbage and human waste. Thanks to these changes, litter problems on Everest are improving.

Efforts are also being made to protect trees in the Everest area. National parks now preserve existing trees, and new trees are being planted. Power plants are also being built around the Everest region. These plants will someday provide new sources of energy for the people who live around

Ang Phurba, the leader of the Everest Rejuvenation Campaign, displays empty oxygen tanks that have been taken from the slopes of Mount Everest.

Two members of a Japanese cleanup expedition sort through some of the 3,500 pounds of trash the team collected from Mount Everest.

Mount Everest. Changes such as these should reduce the demand for firewood and help to save the area's forests.

Today, governments and climbers alike understand that the Everest environment is fragile and must be protected. There is still much work to be done, but remarkable progress has been made since the early 1990s. If this trend continues, there is every hope that climbers can continue to enjoy the world's highest mountain without destroying it in the process.

Glossary

acclimatization: The slow adjustment process that lets climbers get used to increased altitude.

continental drift: A geological process that causes continents to change their positions over time.

dehydration: Loss of water from the body.

elevation: Height above sea level.

erosion: The wearing away of solid substances by wind, rain, and other natural forces.

GPS: Global positioning system; GPS technology can pinpoint the exact position of anything on Earth.

mountaineer: A person who climbs mountains for sport.

refraction: The bending of light as it passes through substances of different thicknesses.

snowline: The elevation on a mountain above which snow never melts.

summit: The highest point of a mountain.

terrain: The physical features of a land area.

theodolite: A telescope that precisely measures angles.

For Further Exploration

Books

Jonathan Chester, *Young Adventurer's Guide to Everest: From Avalanche to Zopkiok*. Berkeley, CA: Tricycle Press, 2002. This book examines Everest topics from A to Z. Read about avalanches, frostbite, and more.

Steve Jenkins, *The Top of the World: Climbing Mount Everest*. Boston, MA: Houghton Mifflin, 1999. Great illustrations and text explain the route to the summit of Everest.

Jon Krakauer, *Into Thin Air*. New York: Anchor Books, 1998. The author describes his experiences in a 1995 storm that killed twelve Everest climbers. For advanced readers.

Thomas Locker, *Mountain Dance*. San Diego, CA: Silver Whistle/Harcourt, 2001. Text and illustrations explain the processes that make and destroy mountains.

Patricia D. Netzley, *Life on an Everest Expedition*. San Diego, CA: Lucent Books, 2001. Learn about the grim realities of daily life on an Everest expedition.

Mark Pfetzer, *Within Reach: My Everest Story*. New York: Dutton Books, 1998. The teenage author of this book tells about his mountain-climbing adventures, including two attempts on Everest.

Websites

Everest News (www.everestnews.com). The main source of Everest information on the web. Includes daily updates from teams currently climbing the mountain.

Kids' Everest Questions (www.cbc.ca). On this site, experts answer kids' questions about Everest. Includes a link to submit new questions.

Index